DATE DUE			
DEC 17 '94			
APR 13 '95			
MAY 15 '95			
FEB 10 '99			

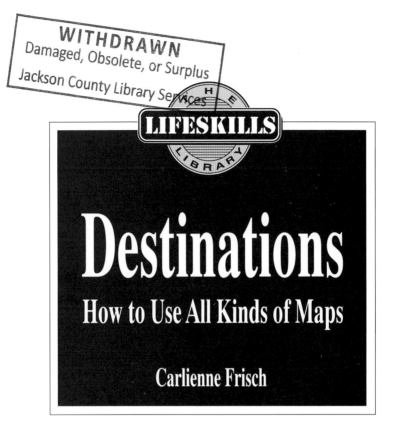

THE LIFESKILLS LIBRARY

Destinations
How to Use All Kinds of Maps

Carlienne Frisch

THE ROSEN PUBLISHING GROUP, INC.

NEW YORK

Published in 1994 by The Rosen Publishing Group, Inc.
29 East 21st Street, New York, NY 10010

First Edition
Copyright 1994 by The Rosen Publishing Group, Inc.

Manufactured in the United States of America

Library of Congress Cataloging-in-Publication Data

Frisch, Carlienne.
    Destination: how to use all kinds of maps / Carlienne Frisch—1st ed.
        p.   cm.
    Includes bibliographical references and index.
    Summary: Discusses how to interpret and use the information found on maps.
    ISBN 0-8239-1607-3
    1. Maps—Juvenile literature. [1. Maps.] I. Title.
    GA130.F75   1993
        912—dc20   93-10577
                                                                              CIP
                                                                              AC

CONTENTS

INTRODUCTION

We go many places. We ride the bus or subway downtown or to other neighborhoods. We visit friends in other cities. We go on vacation to other states. It's easy to get lost in an unfamiliar place. Wherever we are, we can use maps to find our way.

There are many kinds of maps. They are used for different purposes. If you want to find the nearest park, you need a map of your town or city. A map of bus routes will help you visit a friend on the other side of town. A road map will help you find your way on vacation.

In the following chapters, we will learn about different kinds of maps, how to use a map, how to understand map language, and other ideas to help us find our way around. When we finish reading, we will know how to read a map. We will be ready to travel across town or across the country.

You can find your way around town or around the world, using the correct map.

WHAT IS A MAP?

A map is usually a drawing of the world or a part of it. Let's imagine that we are flying over an area. We take a photograph of what we see below and then print a large copy of it. We have made a photographic map. It shows us the direction to get to one place from another. We know whether we must go east or west (right or left) from where we are. The map also shows us distance. We see that some places are close to each other while others are farther apart.

Following a map to get where we want to go is not a new idea. If we had lived in the days of cavemen, we would have drawn maps on sand, rocks, or animal skins. We would have drawn lines to show direction and symbols or signs to show distance. If we drew five suns between two mountain peaks, we would be saying that it took five days to walk from one mountain to the other. Cave dwellers used such maps to find food, water, good hunting grounds, and the way back home.

People across the world have always used maps to travel from place to place. The ancient Babylonians scratched maps on clay tablets. The Chinese painted maps on silk cloth. People who lived on islands in the Pacific Ocean wove maps of reeds and palm leaves. They attached seashells to show where larger islands were located.

Early mapmakers thought the earth was flat. They drew maps guessing about places that no one had yet seen. If we had followed one of their maps, we would have seen unknown areas filled with drawings of monsters and sea serpents. We would probably have been afraid to go beyond the known parts of the world.

If we had lived about 500 years ago, we could have used the first globes. When people learned that the earth is round, they made globes that were incomplete and had many mistakes. As people explored more of the world, globes and maps be-came more accurate.

Kinds of Maps

Today's maps give a clear picture of what our world looks like, from the neighborhood park to the inter-state highway system. We can use maps of ocean depths, the moon's surface, and the solar system.

Local maps show us where schools, libraries, parks, and hospitals are. Airline maps tell us the shortest and fastest way to fly from one city to another. Other maps tell us what time it is in another part of our country or another part of the world.

Almost everyone uses maps. Business people use maps to find good places to sell their products. Military forces use maps to plan strategy. Here is an example of one family's use of a map.

Mike Hansen helps his family to plan a vacation. He opens the road map of South Dakota, the state where the Hansens live. He knows that north is at the top of a map and south is at the bottom. East is to the right and west to the left.

Mike looks at the names of the neighboring states in parentheses on the edges of the map to see what other maps he will need for the family to travel beyond South Dakota. Mike sees that he will need a map of North Dakota because the family want to drive north. The Hansens also plan to visit the states that are west of South Dakota. Looking at the left side of the map, Mike sees that two states border South Dakota on the west—Montana and Wyoming.

Mike calls a travel agency in his town to ask for maps of North Dakota, Montana, and Wyoming. Next year, when the family go south and east on vacation, Mike will ask for maps of Minnesota, Iowa, and Nebraska.

It's fun to help plan a trip. A map will help to get you there, and point out some places of interest along the way.

CHAPTER 2

HOW TO USE MAPS

There are many kinds of maps. Some are general maps, such as a map of Africa or a state highway map. Others are special maps. They show a certain feature of an area, such as population or weather. You must have the right map to find out what you want to know. If you plan to visit Mike Hansen, you need a highway map that shows how to get from your state to South Dakota. But you do not need a map of Japan or of the stars in the heavens. Let's look at different kinds of maps.

The Globe

A *globe* is a round ball, just like the earth. On the globe is a map of the earth's surface. A globe shows the true size, shape, and location of all parts of the earth, just as an astronaut in space would see it. The astronaut can see that the earth tips at a slight angle. A globe is placed in a holder or frame at that same angle.

To see how the globe is like the earth, you can do the experiment that Mike's sister Jenny did. Jenny took a large flashlight to school. In geography class, she pointed the light at the globe, pretending the light was the sun. As Jenny slowly turned the globe in its holder, she saw how each part of the globe moved past the light. When one half of the globe was lit, the other half was dark. One half of the earth gets daylight from the sun while the other half is in darkness. It is important to keep this in mind when you look at a flat map of the world.

There are two kinds of globes: *celestial globes* and *terrestrial globes*. A celestial globe shows the stars and planets. On a terrestrial globe you can see the continents and the oceans, lakes, and other bodies of water.

Terrestrial Globes

There are two kinds of terrestrial globes: *physical* and *political*. A physical globe shows the earth as it looks from an airplane or a satellite. You can see high mountains, flat deserts, and blue oceans. Some physical globes are textured so you can feel the built-up roughness of mountain chains and the smoothness of flat lands. These are called *raised-relief* globes. A globe that shows the height and depth of land that is under water is called a *hydro-graphic-relief* globe. It shows where the underseas mountains are located.

A political globe also has colors for land and water areas. Water is usually a shade of blue. Different colors are used on the land areas to show the outlines of countries.

Let's look at North America on a political globe. One political globe may show the United States as orange. Our northern neighbor, Canada, may be green, and Mexico, our southern neighbor, may be blue. On another political globe the United States may be purple, Canada pink, and Mexico yellow. The specific colors have no meaning. They only help us see the borders between countries or states.

A Globe or a Map?

A globe gives an almost perfect picture of the world, but it has disadvantages. We can see only half of a globe at a time. It is too small to show details. That is why most people look at maps that are printed on paper. A flat map is easier to use because you can see all of it at the same time. The map can show more details. A map is easy to carry with you.

But maps have disadvantages, too. A flat map is a *projection* of the globe's surface onto paper. It is as if the mapmaker had taken a globe and flattened it

———

Students may find it easier using a globe to visualize the world they live in.

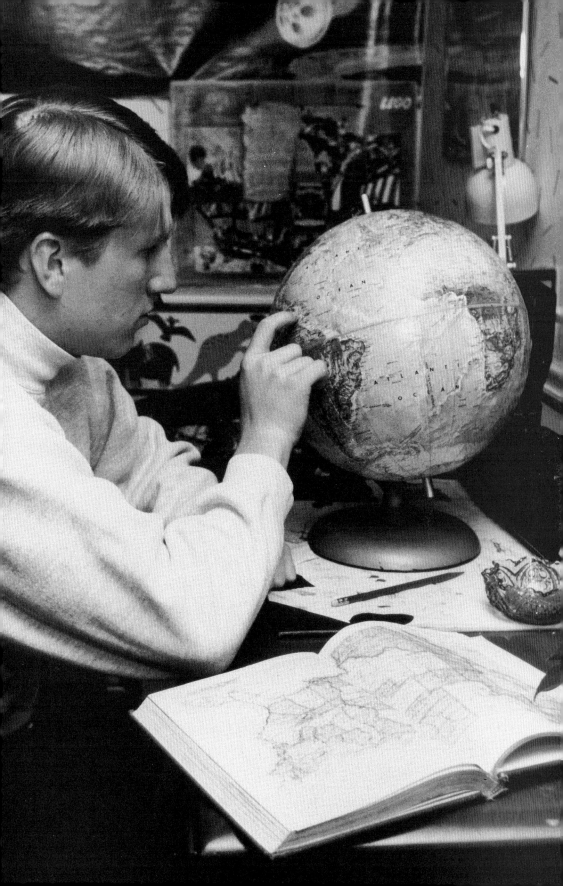

out. It is impossible to take a round surface and make it perfectly flat. That is why all maps have some *distortion*, or inaccuracy. That means that a certain part of the map is not exactly like the part of the world it shows. The greatest distortion is at the top and bottom of the map. Distortion is worse on maps that show a large area. The distortion is very slight on a map of your city because a city is a very small part of the entire globe.

Some maps are printed in a way that prevents distortion. They look like sections cut apart and connected at only a few points. And that is what they are. The only way to put all the pieces together is to put them on a ball—a globe.

The Atlas

An atlas is our passport to the world. It is a book filled with maps. We can learn many things from the maps in an atlas. We can look up what kind of weather is common in the country where our great-grandparents were born. We can find the name of the river near the town where our great-grand-mother grew up. We can learn how many people now live in the town.

The first few pages of an atlas help us to use the book. There we find out what kinds of maps are in the atlas and how to use the information on each page. In the back of the atlas is an index. The index is an alphabetical list of all the places in the atlas and the number of the page on which we can find each one. We will learn more about using this information in later chapters.

Physical-Relief Maps

Most atlases include *physical-relief* maps. This kind of map shows the world the same way as a physical globe except that the map is flat. It shows the natural features of the land, such as jungles, deserts, and mountains. Shadings of color are used to show *elevation*, or height, above sea level. They also show *depression*, or depth below sea level.

Political Maps

A *political map* shows the capital cities and national borders of countries, just as a political globe does. The map makes it easy for us to see where one country ends and another begins. Each country is a different color from its neighbors. Different symbols are used to show which cities and towns are most important. The location of a capital city is usually shown with a star. Other major cities may be marked by a dot within a circle. A circle without a dot marks a smaller city. Some political maps also show highways, railroads, and airplane routes.

Some maps combine the information on a physical map with the information on a political map. This kind of map is called a *physical-political* map. It shows the land's natural features, the boundaries between countries, and other important data.

Product Maps

If we want to know about the farming or industry of an area or a country we can look at a *product* map. This kind of map uses special drawings, called *symbols*, to show where each kind of product is grown on the land or made in a factory. A product map of the United States shows drawings of many kinds of products. We may see drawings of oil wells in the state of Texas, cows in Wisconsin, wheat in North Dakota, and oranges in Florida. From that we can learn that Texas produces oil, that milk is a major product of Wisconsin, that North Dakota grows wheat, and that oranges are a Florida crop.

Transportation Maps

The most common *transportation map* is the road map, or highway map. It is used by drivers to help them travel outside of their community. Other transportation maps, such as street maps and maps that show bus and subway routes, help people find their way within a community.

A road map shows the routes and identification numbers of interstate highways, state roads, and county roads. It also shows on which roads the cities and towns are located. Symbols are used on the map to represent different kinds of roads. The symbol for an interstate highway is a triangular shield with the highway number printed on it.

——

Keep a road map handy whenever you travel far from home.

Other national highways are shown by a number on a sign that looks like a sheriff's badge. State highways and other roads usually have the number printed in a square. The symbol for each kind of road is the same as the highway sign you will see when you travel on the road.

When Mike Hansen helped his family plan their vacation, he learned from the South Dakota road map that they could take U.S. Highway 14 west from their home in Pierre to Interstate Highway 90, which would take them farther west into Wyoming.

Mike's geography teacher told him that names of highways are sometimes shortened. For example, I-90 is really Interstate Highway 90. She also told Mike that when an interstate highway goes through a large city, there is usually another road, a bypass, off the highway that is used to travel around the city. The bypass often has an extra number in front of the highway's number. A bypass on I-90 might be numbered 390 in one large city and 590 in another city. Drivers who take the bypass come back to the regular highway on the other side of the city.

On the back of many road maps are small maps of the state's largest cities. These maps show the major streets and roads in each city and sometimes its suburbs. They help us find our way to the downtown area or to a suburb. But they do not show us all the streets in the city. For that we need a city map. The city map also shows the location of government buildings, hospitals, schools, libraries, museums, parks, zoos, bridges, and airports.

Some cities have public transportation, such as buses or subways. People who use the public transportation need a map to see which bus or subway will take them where they want to go. Route maps are usually posted on the walls of subway stations and at some bus stops. The routes are marked on the map in different colors so passengers can easily see which bus or subway they should take.

Special-Purpose Maps

Scientists who study the stars and planets are called astronomers. They use *maps of the universe* that show millions of galaxies (groups of stars), including the Milky Way galaxy in which the earth is. They use maps of our solar system, which show the sun and the nine planets, including the earth. Some maps also show the orbits, or paths, of the moons that circle around some planets. Other maps show the surface of the moon.

Many other kinds of maps are used for special purposes, too. These include historical or antique maps, nautical charts, air maps, meteorological maps, cartograms, topographical maps, plat maps, and blueprints. Let's see how these maps are used.

Historical Maps

The names of some countries and cities have changed through time. So have the boundaries of many countries. If we want to see what the world

looked like 300 years ago, we must look at *historical* or *antique maps*. There are two kinds of historical maps. Some were made in the past. They show how the world was or how people thought it was. Historical maps that have been made recently show how an area looked in the past. Both have the same kind of information.

When Mike wrote a history report about Germany, he used a historical map to learn what the many parts of the country were called in the 1800s.

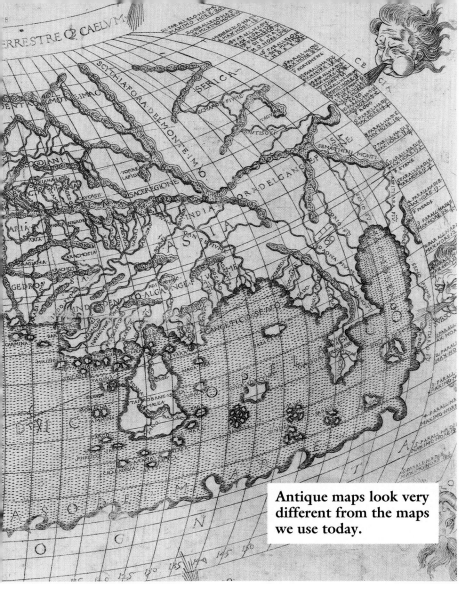

Antique maps look very different from the maps we use today.

Jenny used a historical map to learn more about her genealogy (family history). She knew the names of the European towns in which her great-grandparents grew up. But she could not find those names on a current map of Europe. So she used the index on a historical map to learn the location of the towns. Then she found them on the historical map and looked in the same place on a modern map. She saw that the towns were still there but had different names.

Other Maps

Sailors have always used maps of the seas, called *nautical charts* or *navigational maps.* These show the depth of the water and the ocean currents. They also show land areas such as coastlines, islands, and reefs. They show where lighthouses and buoys are located. Some charts are updated often to show the latest information about icebergs and the stormy areas and winds that change with the seasons.

Pilots use *air maps* or *flyways.* These maps show landmarks such as rivers that help the pilots of small planes stay on course. Pilots of large planes do not need air maps because they follow the instruments in the cockpit of the plane.

Weather forecasters use *meteorological maps* to keep track of air temperature, wind speed and direction, air pressure, moisture, and clouds. Many meteorological maps are printed on computer by the National Weather Service. Your TV station and newspaper use these maps to show you what kind of weather to expect in the next few days.

Cartograms

One kind of map does not show the earth's surface as it really is. It is called a *cartogram.* This kind of map shows only one kind of information, such as the population of each country of the world.

It is important to know that a cartogram does not show countries in their correct sizes. A population cartogram shows Japan as about half the size of the United States. But you know from geography class that Japan is a very small country. Why does the cartogram show Japan so large? A population cartogram shows the countries with the most people as the largest. Countries with the fewest people are drawn the smallest. Japan has about half as many people as the United States, so it is drawn half as large as the United States. If Japan and the United States had the same population, they would be drawn the same size on the map.

If you want to go hiking or backpacking, you will want a *topographical map* that shows the natural and man-made features of the earth's surface. A large-scale (or close-up) topographical map shows many details. It may even show each building on a street.

If you were interested in buying land outside of a city or town, you could use a *plat map* to find out who owned the property. Plat maps show the outlines of each piece of property in an area such as a county. The name of each property owner or resident is printed within the outline of the property. Plat maps show even the smallest roads, which do not appear on state road maps. People who deliver packages throughout the country use plat maps to see where they need to go.

Another kind of detailed map is called a *blueprint*. Construction workers use blueprints in making a building. It shows the workers where such things as electrical wires and outlets and plumbing pipes are supposed to go.

WHAT MAPS TELL

Reading a map is like reading a book. When you see the symbols (letters) *c-o-w* in a story, you know they refer to a large farm animal. Once you know what the symbols on a map mean, you will be able to "read" the map. The story of the map contains five "Ds": description, direction, designations, details, and distance.

Description

The name of the area the map covers, such as a state or city, is called the *description*. It is printed at the top and bottom of the map. The date when the map was printed is also at the bottom. Unless you want historical data, you should use an up-to-date map to be sure the information is current.

Maps of city bus routes are often posted at bus stops.

Direction

Maps also show *direction*, which means "which way." When you hold a map so that the printing is right side up, *north* is at the top and *south* at the bottom. North is the direction toward the North Pole from any other place on earth. South is just the opposite—the direction from any place on earth toward the South Pole. With the map in this position, *east* is on your right and *west* on your left. If the place you want to go is above and to the left of where you are on the map, you will travel north and west, or northwest, to get there.

Most maps have a symbol called a *compass rose*. It is a small design, usually in the shape of a circle, with points around the edge. At the top is the longest point. It shows which direction is north.

Most maps have numbers printed in the margin across the top of the map. The same numbers are printed in the bottom margin. Along the sides, in the left and right margins, are letters in alphabetical order. These letters and numbers will help you find a certain place on the map.

When you look in the map's *index*, or alphabetical list of places, you will see a number and a letter after each place. These numbers and letters tell you where to find that place on the map. If you want to find the city where Mike and Jenny Hansen live, you look at the index on a South Dakota highway map. You run down the index until you find the "P"s. You find Pierre listed between Pierpont and

Pine Ridge. The index will look something like this:

Pierpont, 184 . . . . B-15
Pierre, 12,032. . . . . D-11
Pine Ridge, 3,059. . . . . . G-8

The number right after the name of each city or town is the number of people who live there. Can you tell how many people live in Pierre? If you said, "About 12,000," you are correct. The exact number was 12,032 when the map was printed.

The letter and number at the far right show where you can find the city or town on the map. Pierre is where the letter "D" and the number "11" meet on the map. Let's see how this works.

Run your finger down the left or right side of the map until you come to the letter "D." Then run your other hand across the top or bottom until you come to the number "11." Now slide the "D" finger across the map until it is below the "11" finger. Bring the "11" finger down to meet the "D" finger. Look for the name of the city, Pierre, near the spot where your fingers meet.

Designations

Maps have signs called *symbols*. They show where man-made things are located. All maps have a printed *legend* or *key*, usually in one corner of the map. The key tells what the symbols *designate* or show. The symbols usually are black drawings, but

some are red or other colors. Next to each drawing
is the name of the thing it represents. On a road
map, superhighways may be shown by thick lines,
and two-lane highways by a thinner line. A gravel
road is usually shown as a dotted line. The key
shows you what kind of drawing represents each
detail, such as a bridge, a school, or a library.

A symbol looks like the thing it represents. The
drawing of an airplane in an outlined area means an
airport. A cemetery may be shown by a cross drawn
inside a square. A drawing of a tent means a camp-
ground. A railroad track is shown as a continuous
line with short lines crossing it.

Details

Color is an important detail on a map. The lines
marking different kinds of roads are different colors.
Rivers are shown as blue lines. Oceans, lakes, and
other large water areas are also blue. Ice caps are
white, forests are dark green, grasslands are light
green, deserts are yellow, and farmlands are brown.

Colors also are used on maps to show differences
in rainfall and temperature. Television weather
reports often show temperature maps. The area
of the country that has the hottest temperatures
(usually over 100 degrees) is colored red. The next
hottest area (temperatures in the 90s) is orange.
Yellow shows the area with temperatures in the 80s.

—

**Many outdoor facilities such as parks, zoos, and amusement
centers provide maps of the grounds and surrounding areas.**

Green stands for temperatures in the 70s. In the winter, when temperatures are lower, you will see mostly greens, blues, and purples on the TV weather map.

A map that tells us where it is raining or snowing shows all of the dry areas in one color, such as orange. The rainy areas are a different color, such as bright blue. The next time you watch a weather report on TV, notice how color is used to show different weather patterns.

Some newspapers also print weather maps in color. These maps look much like the weather maps you see on TV. But a black-and-white weather map may show differences in temperature by using shades of black and gray. The hottest part of the country may be colored black. The next hottest area will be dark gray. A cooler area will be light gray. The coolest area will be white or a very light shade of gray. Rain may be shown as slanted lines across an area. Snow may be shown as dots. The key printed next to the map will show you what the shadings and other symbols represent.

Distance

Maps also show us *distance*, or how far it is from one place to another. To find the distance between two places on a map, you need to know the map's *scale*. This is the difference between real distances and how far apart they are on the map. Each inch on a map stands for a certain distance on the earth.

Scale is usually shown in large numbers, so you may think that understanding it is difficult. But it is easy to figure out scale with a ruler.

On a map of the world, one inch might stand for a distance of 1,000 miles. There are 5,280 feet in a mile, and 12 inches in a foot; 5,280 times 12 equals 63,360,000 inches. So the map key will show the scale as 1:63,360,000. But the key will also show that one inch on the map is equal to 1,000 miles. That makes it much easier to understand scale and to figure distance.

To find the distance between two cities, you can measure the distance on the map with a ruler and multiply that distance by 1,000 miles. For example, if on your map the city where you live measures two inches from the city where Mike and Jenny live, you multiply two inches by 1,000 miles to learn that the cities are 2,000 miles apart.

If the key shows that an inch equals 100 miles, and the cities are five inches apart on the map, can you figure the real distance between the cities? You should multiply the distance on the map (five inches) by the number of miles per inch (100). The answer is 500. Now you know that the real distance between the two cities is 500 miles.

A map that covers a large area, such as a world map, shows distances on a small scale. A map that covers a smaller area, such as a road map, shows distances on a larger scale. A city street map is drawn to even larger scale because it shows a small part of the world.

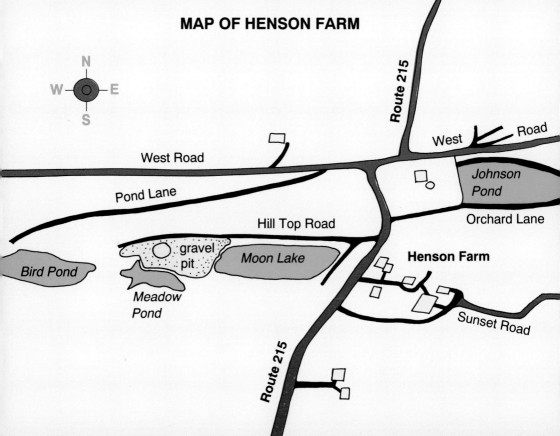

MAP OF HENSON FARM

N
W E
S

Route 215

West Road

West Road

Pond Lane

Johnson Pond

Orchard Lane

Hill Top Road

gravel pit

Bird Pond

Moon Lake

Meadow Pond

Henson Farm

Sunset Road

Route 215

UNDERSTANDING
MAP LANGUAGE

We know that physical-relief maps and topographical maps show the height above the surface of the earth. This elevation is indicated with color and with *contour lines.*

Maps that show elevation by color use one color for all land areas that are at the same elevation. For example, land at sea level will be green. The next level of elevation will be colored yellow. Hilly areas will be tan, and mountainous areas will be brown.

The depth of water areas is shown the same way. For example, the shallow parts of the ocean, such as along the shore, are colored light blue. Dark blue shows where the ocean is deepest.

Some maps show elevation with contour lines. These are imaginary lines that look like slices of the

—

An aerial view (top) can be translated into a drawing of a map (bottom) which gives more information.

earth or rings in a bathtub. Each line is exactly the same distance above sea level. The lowest contour line may stand for land that is 30 feet above sea level. The next line will stand for land that is at 60 feet, and so on. A number printed on each contour line tells the elevation.

It is easy to see where land is steep even without reading the numbers. When the contour lines are far apart, the land is flat. When the lines are close together, the land is steep. The lines that show a steep cliff, for example, will be nearly on top of one another.

The Equator

Imaginary lines are also used to show the exact location of every place on earth. The lines run from three locations: the *North Pole* at the top of the earth, the *South Pole* at the bottom of the earth, and the *equator*.

The equator is an imaginary line, 25,000 miles long. It runs around the middle of the earth at the widest part. The equator is an equal distance from the North and South Poles. It divides the earth into two equal parts called *hemispheres*. The Northern Hemisphere is the half of the earth that is above or north of the equator. The lower or southern half of the earth is called the Southern Hemisphere.

The imaginary lines that run from east to west—in the same direction as the equator—are called *latitude lines* or *parallels*. They show how far north or south a place is from the equator. Latitude is measured in *degrees* (°). The degrees on a map do not show temperature. They show distance.

The equator is at 0°. The first line above it is at 10° north. The next line is at 20°, and so on to the North Pole, which is at 90° north. Degrees are measured the same way below the equator, with the first line at 10° south and the South Pole at 90° south. On large-scale maps, latitude lines may be drawn at each degree.

Meridians

Imaginary lines also run up and down the earth from the North Pole to the South Pole. They are called *longitude lines* or *meridians.* Longitude also is measured in degrees. The point from which it is measured is the imaginary line drawn through Greenwich, England. This line is called the *Green-wich meridian* or *prime meridian.* Meridians are east or west of the Greenwich meridian. Those that are east of it show the distance around the earth in the Eastern Hemisphere. This hemisphere includes the continents of Europe, Asia, Africa, and Australia. The meridians of west longitude measure the distance halfway around the earth in the opposite direction. They are in the Western Hemisphere. This includes North America, South America, and part of the Pacific Ocean.

East and west meridians meet at the 180° meridian, which is called the *international date line.* Its purpose is to even out the time gained or lost by people who travel through several time zones. The date to the east of the line is one day earlier than to the west of the line. We will learn more about time zones a few pages further on.

Coordinates

Latitude lines cross the earth sideways. Longitude lines run from the earth's top to its bottom. The lines cross in many places on a map of the earth. They form a *global grid* or pattern of squares. These squares can be numbered with degrees of latitude and degrees of longitude. Each of these numbers is called a *coordinate*. The degree of latitude is always written first.

Let's learn how to find the latitude and longitude of a particular place on a map. Here's how Jenny Hansen did it. In her school library, Jenny turned to the index at the back of the atlas. She looked up her home city, Pierre, South Dakota, and turned to the map of the north central United States.

The latitude lines were drawn one degree apart. Degree numbers were printed on each latitude line at the right and left edges of the map. Jenny learned that the northern border of her state was about 46° north of the equator. The 44° line was a short distance south of Pierre, so she decided that Pierre was about 44° north of the equator.

To find longitude, Jenny looked at the degrees printed at the top and bottom of the map. The

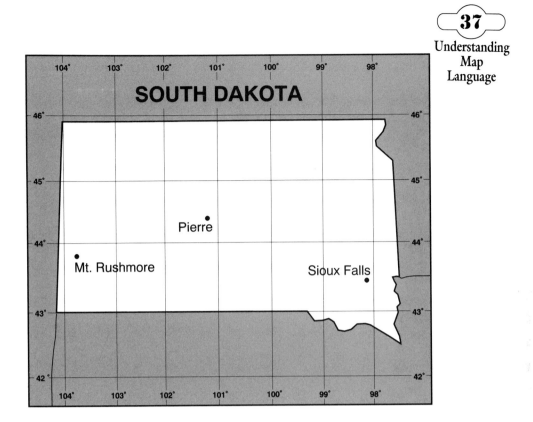

SOUTH DAKOTA

101° longitude line ran down the map just east of
Pierre. Jenny knew that Pierre was about 101° west
of the Greenwich meridian. She wrote down 44°N,
101°W as the coordinates of Pierre, South Dakota.

There are smaller divisions of degrees. These
divisions are called *minutes* and *seconds*. They measure distance, not time. A minute is 1/60 of a
degree. A second is 1/60 of a minute or 1/360 of
a degree. Minutes are shown by the symbol ('), and
seconds by the symbol (").

By using these symbols we can be even more
exact in stating the coordinates of a place. To do
this, Jenny looked in a different atlas and found a
map that showed minutes. She learned that the
latitude for Pierre was actually 44° 18'.

Time Zones

Meridians also divide the earth into 24 areas called *time zones.* The people living in each time zone use the same clock time. The zones are set at 15° sections east or west of the prime meridian. This is because the earth takes 24 hours to complete a turn of 360°. If you divide 360° by 24 hours, you learn that the earth turns at the rate of 15° per hour. The sun reaches a new time zone every hour.

The continental United States has four time zones. New York is in the zone with the latest time. Los Angeles is in the zone with the earliest time. The time in Los Angeles is three hours earlier than in New York. It is two hours earlier than in Chicago, and one hour earlier than in Denver. You can see that if you travel from Chicago to Los Angeles, you "gain" two hours. Because the states of Alaska and Hawaii are farther away, they are in separate time zones.

Many maps that cover a large area show time zones. A meridian marks the center of each time zone. This means that each time zone runs seven and one half degrees on either side of a meridian. If you look at a map of the world, you see that the lines of time zones are not straight lines from north to south like meridian lines. Time zones bend and curve around because it would be inconvenient to split a city or even a small country into two time zones.

HELPFUL HINTS

Before you go on a trip, decide where you want to go and get all the maps you will need. Take the time to study each map. At the end of this chapter you will find a list of places where you can get maps.

When you have the maps you need, spread them out on a table. Plan your route. Sometimes the shortest way is not always the most interesting. If you have the time, another longer route might be more fun.

You can mark your map with a crayon or colored marker. If you use a color that is not printed on the map, your route will be easy to see. Be sure to take your map with you, but do not read the map while driving or walking. Stop out of the way of traffic before taking a look at your map.

Other Uses of Maps

When you think of maps, you probably think of traveling. But you can use maps for other things. Of course, maps are helpful in geography, social studies, history, and civics classes. But you can also use a map in a report for music or art class. You can show your classmates a map of the country or state in which a famous musician or artist began his or her career. You can use maps in home economics class to show the countries where certain foods are grown. Your classmates will understand any report better with visual aid.

You can use maps on directories in malls to find a store or to figure out where you are. You can also draw maps. For instance, you want to bring a computer desk into your room but are not sure where to put it. There doesn't seem to be much extra space. You draw a map of your room and note the placement of each piece of furniture. You discover on your map that there is space against one wall, but you didn't notice it before because the room was too cluttered.

There are many places to get maps. You can check a map out from the library. You should not write or draw on a library map. You can buy road maps at service stations. For a school report, you can photocopy a map from a book and color the different areas to match it. You can even draw your own map, such as a map of your neighborhood.

—

A floor plan is a map of a room. This is helpful when planning furniture arrangements.

You can ask for maps from many government agencies. Some of the maps are free, but there is a charge for others. Here is a list of a few agencies and the kinds of maps they have. When you write to an agency, explain what kind of map you want and how you plan to use it (for a school report or vacation). Ask if there is a charge for the map. Be sure to print your name, complete address, and phone number including area code.

Library of Congress
101 Independence Avenue S.E.
Washington, DC 20540
(Maps, atlases, and globes)

Defense Mapping Agency
Building 56
U.S. Naval Observatory
Washington, DC 20305-3000
(Topographic maps, nautical charts, moon and planetary maps, and military maps)

Public Affairs Office
U.S. Forest Service
U.S. Dept. of Agriculture
P.O. Box 96090
Washington, DC 20090-6090
(National forest maps and recreation maps)

Public Affairs Office
U.S. Geological Survey
Department of the Interior
119 National Center
Reston, VA 22092
(Topographic maps, county maps, regional maps, state maps, United States maps, polar region maps, moon and planetary maps, federal water resource maps, river survey maps, mineral and energy resource maps, the National Atlas, and land use maps)

Central Intelligence Agency
Washington, DC 20505
(Country and world maps)

Wherever your travels take you, maps add to the pleasure and excitement of your journey. Use them and have a safe trip.

ORIENTEERING

"Give me a map and I'm magic." That's the orienteer's slogan. An orienteer is a person who takes part in a sport called *orienteering*. The sport is usually held in a rough, wooded area, but it can be played on city streets or in a mall. Orienteers use a map of the area to find a series of places called *control points* where each player's entry card is punched or signed. The points are shown on the map by flags or other markers. Each orienteer is assigned a certain order in which to go to the control points. Because everyone in the race follows a different course to the final control point, it is not a good idea to follow another orienteer. Players run, jog, or walk. The person who finishes the course correctly in the shortest time wins.

Orienteering was invented in Sweden in 1918 by Major Ernst Killander. It became popular in the United States in the 1970s. Some courses are as short as a mile, with four control points. Others may be eight miles long, with 75 control points. Most orienteers, especially those on outdoor courses, use a *compass* as well as a map. A compass is a small, round instrument with a magnetized needle that always points north. It helps map readers know the direction they are facing so they can turn their maps in the same direction.

GLOSSARY
EXPLAINING NEW WORDS

atlas A book of maps.

blueprint A map that shows the construction of a building.

cartogram A map that shows only one kind of information, usually by size, dots, or shaded areas.

celestial globe A globe that shows the stars and planets.

compass rose Map symbol that points north.

contour lines Lines on a map that show height above sea level.

coordinate The degree of latitude or the degree of longitude used to locate a place on a map.

degree One of the 360 units of measure that make up a circle, shown by the symbol (°).

depression Distance below sea level.

distortion The inaccuracy caused by the map's projection.

Eastern Hemisphere The half of the earth that includes Europe, Asia, Africa, and Australia.

elevation Height above sea level.

equator Imaginary circle drawn around the middle of the earth.

globe A sphere-shaped model of the earth.

index An alphabetical list.

international date line Imaginary line of longitude at which the date becomes one day earlier on the east of the line.

latitude Distance north or south, using imaginary lines running in the same direction as the equator.

legend The part of a map that lists and explains the symbols used.

longitude Distance east or west, using imaginary lines that run between the North and South Poles.

map projection A way of showing the earth's curved surface on a flat sheet of paper.

meridian An imaginary line of longitude that runs between the North Pole and South Pole.

meteorological map A map that shows the weather.

nautical chart A map of the water, used by sailors.

physical-relief map A map that shows the earth's natural features.

plat map A map that shows the outlines of properties and the owners' names.

Poles, North and South Imaginary points at the northern and southern ends of the earth, at 90°.

political map or globe A map or globe that shows capital cities, countries, or states.

scale The difference between real distances and how they appear on a map.

symbol A written or printed mark, picture, or sign that stands for something else.

terrestrial globe A globe of the earth.

time zone 24 areas of the earth in which the time is one hour later than in the previous zone.

topographical Map showing natural and man-made features.

Western Hemisphere The half of the earth that includes North America and South America.

FOR FURTHER READING

Carey, Helen H. *How to Use Maps and Globes.* New York: Franklin Watts, 1983.

Carlisle, Norman and Madelyn. *The True Book of Maps.* Chicago: Childrens Press, 1969.

Fuchs, Erich. *Looking at Maps.* New York: Abelard-Schuman, 1976.

Kjellstrom, Bjorn. *Be Expert with Map and Compass: The Orienteering Handbook.* New York: Charles Scribner's Sons, 1976.

Knowlton, Jack. *Maps and Globes.* New York: HarperCollins Children's Books, 1985.

Lambert, David. *Maps and Globes.* New York: The Bookwright Press, 1987.

Madden, James F. *The Wonderful World of Maps.* Maplewood, NJ: Hammond, Inc., 1982.

Weiss, Harvey. *Maps: Getting from Here to There.* Boston: Houghton Mifflin Co., 1991.

INDEX

About the Author

Carlienne Frisch has written books on such diverse topics as pet care, European countries, and the author Maud Hart Lovelace. Before becoming a free-lance writer, she worked as an editor for a farm magazine and in public relations for nonprofit organizations.

The author is president of the Friends of the Minnesota Valley Regional Library and a member of the Society of Children's Book Writers, Habitat for Humanity, and the local historical society. She enjoys reading mysteries and historical novels. She also collects, decorates, and furnishes dollhouses.

Ms. Frisch and her husband, Robert, have four adult children. They share their home with York, a tortoise-shell cat.

Photo Credits
Cover: Top left, top right, and bottom left by Dru Nadler.
Bottom right by Stuart Rabinowitz.
All photos by Dru Nadler except pages 20–21: Library of Congress;
page 32 (top): Stuart Rabinowitz.

Design & Production by Blackbirch Graphics